Creativity Is Currency Workbook

By

David Toliver

Theempoweredcreators@gmail.com

Reader Acknowledgement

The *Creativity Is Currency Workbook* is an additional resource meant to be used alongside *Creativity Is Currency: How To Turn Your Ideas Into Wealth*, which is a motivational and educational resource designed to inspire personal transformation, creative empowerment, and entrepreneurial action. The strategies, methods, and concepts shared in this book are based on the author's experience, research, and perspective.

While this book provides powerful tools and insights for personal and financial growth, it does not guarantee specific results. Every reader's journey is different. Your success depends on many factors, including your background, effort, commitment, mindset, and timing.

This book is not a substitute for financial, legal, medical, or psychological advice. Please consult the appropriate licensed professional before making any significant changes in these areas.

Editor Acknowledgement

I would like to extend my deepest gratitude to my editor, Emmanuel, whose exceptional skill and insight helped shape this book into its best form. Emmanuel not only honored the vision I carried for this work, but also elevated it. Emmanuel refined the book while preserving its heart and purpose. From the beginning, Emmanuel demonstrated a clear understanding of my goals, offering constructive guidance that never compromised my voice. His editorial precision and thoughtful suggestions made a tremendous impact on the clarity, flow, and effectiveness of every chapter. It was a true collaboration marked by professionalism, integrity, and excellence. I am sincerely grateful for his dedication to this project. Emmanuel, your contribution will always be part of the foundation of *Creativity Is Currency.* It was an honor to work with you. I am sure we will continue a long working relationship, as we give God all the Glory!

— **David Toliver**

Earnings Disclaimer

Any case studies, income examples, or business outcomes discussed in this book are not promises or guarantees of results. They are shared for educational purposes only. There is no assurance you will earn any income by simply reading or applying the methods in this book. Any financial success or transformation you achieve will be the result of your own dedication, consistency, and actions.

Author Disclaimer

I, David Toliver, author of *Creativity Is Currency: How To Turn Your Ideas Into Wealth* and *Creativity Is Currency Workbook*, make every effort to ensure the accuracy of the information presented in this book. However, the content is provided "as is" and without warranties of any kind, either expressed or implied. I assume no responsibility or liability for any errors, omissions, or outcomes that may arise from applying the content of this book.

This book is written to educate, uplift, and encourage creativity and self-leadership. It is not intended to replace personalized coaching, counseling, legal services, or business advice from qualified professionals. You are responsible for your own choices and outcomes.

By reading this book, you agree to take full responsibility for your personal and business decisions.

Table Of Content

Dear Creator,

Before you write in this workbook, pause for a moment. Place both of your hands in front of you. Look at them. These hands have the power to build, create, write, design, lead, serve, restore, and transform. These hands—your hands—are not empty. They are full of potential, packed with stories, experiences, skills, insights, and ideas that the world is waiting to receive.

This workbook is more than a place for notes—it's a sacred space. It is your **launchpad**—a powerful starting point for building something real and meaningful from within. You are not just reading a book; you are stepping into ownership. Chapter One invites you to discover what's already in your possession—the tools, gifts, ideas, and insights you've already been given. You may not have everything you think you need, but you have enough to start.

How to Use This Workbook

This workbook was intentionally created to be:

- **A Reflection Tool** – Use the journal prompts to pause, reflect, and uncover your creativity, values, and untapped abilities.

- **A Strategy Pad** – Jot down real-time ideas, business concepts, or creative sparks that come to mind as you work through the chapter.

- **An Application Guide** – At the end of each section, you'll find space to map out your first steps. These exercises will help you apply what you've learned and move forward with clarity.

- **A Creative Planning Space** – Use the diagrams, benchmarks, and planning pages to visualize your future. Sketch your vision. Write your product idea. Start your outline. This is your space to own it all.

- **A Confidence Builder** – As you document your thoughts, you're training your mindset to believe in your ability to create something that adds value to the world, and can be compensated for it.

What You'll Gain:

By completing this workbook chapter, you will:

- Gain clarity on what you already possess
- Identify the creative assets and ideas you can develop
- Begin designing your unique offering
- Strengthen your sense of ownership and confidence
- Set a foundation for building wealth through your creativity

---

Word to the Reader

This is not about perfection. It's about **ownership**. It's about permitting yourself to start—right now, right where you are—with what you have in your hands. Whether it's an idea, a story, a talent, or a lived experience, **what you hold today can unlock your tomorrow.**

Use this workbook to begin the journey. Let it be a witness to your growth, a journal of your creativity, and a record of the bold steps you will take from here.

"The Fire in the Seed"

From the book: Creativity Is Currency
By David Toliver

There once was a young woman named Jordan. She didn't come from money. No silver spoons, no famous name, and no handouts. What she had was something far more valuable—an idea. A flicker of creativity. A whisper that said, *"Maybe... just maybe... I could create something that matters."*

But like most of us, Jordan was also surrounded by noise—doubtful voices, responsibilities, and a constant feeling that success belonged to someone else. She was stuck between survival and significance. Each day she went to work, gave her best, and wondered if *this* was all life had to offer.

Until one morning, she looked in the mirror and whispered back to the voice in her heart, *"I'm done waiting. I'm going to move—even if I'm scared. I'm going to build—even if I don't know how."*

That was the day her creativity became a *calling.*

That was the day she chose to activate what was in her hands instead of being paralyzed by what she didn't have.

That decision didn't magically open every door. But it did unlock one crucial thing: her mindset.
Jordan began creating, failing, and learning. And building. She treated her creativity like currency. She used her gifts as tools, not decorations. Slowly, her idea evolved into a source of income. Her voice turned into value. And her courage became contagious.

Jordan didn't just change her life—she changed the lives of others. And now, she stands where you stand: on the edge of *possibility.*

Dear Reader,

You are the *creator* in this story.

This book was written for the *Jordan* in you—the dreamer, the builder, the one who has something powerful inside but has been waiting for permission to act.

Let me tell you the truth:

You don't need permission.
You don't need perfection.
You need the courage to begin.

Creativity Is Currency Workbook will show you that you already have what it takes. But more importantly, it will teach you how to *use it.*

This is more than a book. It's a **blueprint**. A **mentor** in your hand. A **wealth map** to follow.

You will learn how to:

- Activate your ideas
- Build a skill set that solves real problems
- Transform your identity and mindset
- Monetize what's in your hands

- Protect your income
- Multiply your impact
- Leave a legacy of influence and wealth

Don't walk in fear. Don't wait until the timing is "perfect." There is greatness in you *right now.* Your Creator didn't make you average. You are more than a conqueror—and the proof is this moment.

You picked up this book. That's the beginning.

Now let's walk together into everything you were born to build.

Faithfully,
David Toliver
Founder & CEO, *Creativity Is Currency*

Creativity Is Currency – Chapter One: Course Material & Workbook

Chapter One Focus: What's In Your Hands?

50 Ways to Activate Ideas That People Will Pay You For

MINDSET SHIFTS (1–10): Start With the Inner Work

1. **Believe your ideas are valuable** – Shift from doubt to belief.
2. **Visualize yourself already succeeding** – See yourself being paid for your creativity.
3. **Declare daily: "I solve problems people pay for"** – Speak it until you live it.
4. **Treat your mind like sacred soil** – Plant only growth-minded thoughts.
5. **Let go of perfectionism** – Clarity comes through motion, not waiting.
6. **Write down one idea a day for 30 days** – Momentum builds mastery.
7. **Study how problems equal opportunities** – Every pain is a paycheck in disguise.
8. **Identify what people always ask your advice on** – That's your gold mine.
9. **Replace "I can't" with "How can I?"** – Solutions begin with better questions.
10. **Ask yourself: "What has life taught me the hard way?"** – Package that lesson.

DISCOVERY TOOLS (11–20): Uncover What You Already Have

11. **Inventory your life experiences** – Turn past struggles into coaching, courses, or books.
12. **Audit your skill set** – What can you teach, fix, or improve?
13. **Create a personal "problem-solver" map** – Link your skills to problems people face.
14. **Make a list of 10 things you're good at** – Bundle them into an offer.
15. **Interview your friends** – Ask what they think you're known for.
16. **Journal about what frustrates you in the world** – Your annoyance is a clue.
17. **Research trending problems in your community or industry**.
18. **Use AI or search engines to explore current market gaps**.
19. **Study reviews of books, tools, or courses in your niche** – Find what's missing.
20. **Reflect on what you've helped someone with for free** – Could that be monetized?

STRATEGIC ACTIVATORS (21–30): Turn Ideas Into Action

21. **Create a problem/solution list** – One column for problems, one for your solutions.
22. **Use the "pain-point prompt"**: What do people complain about daily?
23. **Write your idea in one sentence: "I help [who] do [what] so they can [benefit]."**
24. **Sketch your idea on paper** – Visualization breeds belief.
25. **Pitch your idea to 3 people** – Instant feedback sharpens the concept.

26. **Give away your idea in value (content)** before selling – build trust first.
27. **Break the idea into a system** (3 steps, five pillars, etc.) – Clarity sells.
28. **Design a signature name for it** – Give your idea an identity.
29. **Host a free workshop to test your idea** – Watch what resonates.
30. **Bundle your idea with a transformation** – People pay for outcomes.

PRODUCTIZE & PACKAGE (31–40): Make It Tangible

31. **Turn your idea into a mini course.**
32. **Create a one-page worksheet that solves a problem.**
33. **Develop a "quick win" service offer based on your idea.**
34. **Start a paid challenge around your concept.**
35. **Write an eBook on one key idea.**
36. **Turn your idea into coaching packages.**
37. **Design a masterclass on Zoom and charge admission.**
38. **Create a digital download on Canva or Gumroad.**
39. **Monetize your idea through a subscription (e.g., Patreon, offering email tips or templates).**
40. **Record a podcast episode sharing your idea and its results.**

BOOST & SCALE (41–50): Grow the Idea Into Income

41. **Build a landing page with a call to action.**
42. **Run a paid ad to test your idea.**
43. **Create a waitlist for your product or service.**
44. **Offer beta access in exchange for testimonials.**

45. **Partner with someone who already has your audience**.
46. **Use social proof (quotes, reviews, screenshots)** to build trust.
47. **Bundle the idea into a larger offer (package deal)**.
48. **Create a licensing version of your content** that others can use.
49. **Pitch your idea to podcasts or stages** – get visible.
50. **Keep showing up daily—consistency turns ideas into income.**

Pick up Encouragement:

You're not waiting on permission—you're sitting on power.

Start where you are. Take what's in your hands. Build the idea inside you into something that blesses others, solves actual problems, and funds the vision in your heart.

Start today. Start with one idea.

Reflection: Who Will Benefit Most from Your Creativity?

"The value of your creativity isn't just in what you create—it's in the lives you transform because you dared to create it."

Take a deep breath and ask yourself—who stands to gain the most from what you create?

Your creativity is not just a personal gift; it's a valuable asset. It's a tool for service, transformation, and impact. You were given your ideas for a reason. Inside you is a solution that someone else is waiting for.

Journal Prompts:

1. **Who do you feel called to help?**
   Think about the people who keep showing up in your heart. Are they young entrepreneurs? Single mothers? Underserved youth? Creators struggling to start? Write down your audience.
2. **What specific problem can your creativity solve for them?**
   Is it a lack of confidence? No access to opportunity? Need for education or inspiration? Identify one thing your idea or service could resolve.
3. **What changes will they experience after interacting with your work?**
   Describe the transformation. What does their life look like after your creativity touches it?
4. **What part of your own story would inspire them most?**
   Your testimony is your authority. Reflect on your journey and consider which parts will resonate with and encourage others.
5. **What's stopping you from showing up for them today?**
   Be honest. Is it fear? Doubt? Uncertainty? Name it—and commit to push past it.

Introduction

Title: "What's in Your Hands Today?" – A Launchpad for Action and Ownership

Course Material: Overview

In Chapter One, you are challenged to recognize that you already have tools, skills, resources, and experiences in your hands right now. This course module will help you take inventory, realize your creative potential, and set the foundation for wealth-building through your existing gifts.

Guided Exercises

Exercise 1: Skill Inventory
- List every skill you currently have, no matter how small—examples: writing, organizing, encouraging, designing.

Exercise 2: Resource Discovery
- What resources (tools, contacts, platforms) are already available to you?

Exercise 3: Experience Reflection
- Reflect on three life experiences that taught you a valuable lesson. How could these be turned into a product, service, or solution?

Action Steps

1. Complete the Skill, Resource, and Experience Inventories.
2. Choose one skill or resource that you will commit to developing further.
3. Brainstorm three simple ways the skill could help someone else solve a problem.
4. Create a simple offer or idea using what you already have.

Templates

- Skill Inventory Template: [Skill] | [How It Helps] | [Monetization Ideas]
- Resource Discovery Template: [Resource] | [Access Method] | [Usage Ideas]
- Experience Reflection Template: [Story] | [Lesson] | [Potential Product/Service]

Monetization Checklist

- Do I have a skill that solves a real problem?
- Can I offer a simple service using this skill?

Can I teach this skill to someone else?

- Can I create a product based on my experience?

Is there an audience seeking this solution?

- Can I package my knowledge into a course, guide, or consultation?

Idea-to-Income Framework

Step 1: Identify the Problem You Solve

Step 2: Define Who Needs Your Solution

Step 3: Create a Small Product or Service Based on Your Skill

Step 4: Share It Publicly (Start With Family, Friends, Online)

Step 5: Collect Feedback and Refine

Step 6: Build Systems to Deliver Your Product Consistently

Step 7: Scale With Referrals and Digital Assets

PART 1: 50 Ways to Develop a Distinctive or Specialized Skill Set

These methods are designed to help readers grow in mastery, purpose, and clarity of contribution.

- Personal Mastery

1. **Commit to Daily Learning (30 minutes minimum)**
2. **Master a Specific Tool, Software, or Platform**
3. **Take an Online Certification Course**
4. **Read 1 Book per Month in Your Field**
5. **Attend Mastermind Groups or Skill Circles**
6. **Work with a Mentor or Coach**
7. **Solve a Problem You Struggle With**
8. **Teach What You Know to Someone Else**
9. **Document the Process of Learning Something New**
10. **Shadow Someone Successful in That Skill**

- Creative Application

11. **Start a Passion Project**
12. **Build a Prototype or Demo**
13. **Write Case Studies Based on Hypothetical Clients**
14. **Reverse Engineer a Popular Product/Service**
15. **Use AI Tools to Create Content Ideas and Concepts**
16. **Launch a Weekly Blog or Vlog About Your Process**
17. **Create a Portfolio or Website of Your Work**
18. **Gamify Your Skill Development**
19. **Enter Competitions or Contests in Your Niche**
20. **Create Your Framework or Method**

- Market Research

21. **Survey People in Your Network About Pain Points**

22. **Join Niche Forums or Facebook Groups**
23. **Study the Top 10 People in Your Field**
24. **Write a "Gap in the Market" Report**
25. **Test Skills in Freelance Marketplaces (Upwork, Fiverr)**
26. **Ask Potential Customers: "What's your biggest frustration right now?"**
27. **Read Industry White Papers**
28. **Analyze Amazon/YouTube Reviews in Your Category**
29. **Attend Local or Online Networking Events**
30. **Conduct Informational Interviews with Experts**

- Skill Refinement

31. **Track Progress Weekly with a Skills Journal**
32. **Use Feedback Loops from Peers and Mentors**
33. **Create a Monthly Skill Growth Report**
34. **Set Skill Development SMART Goals**
35. **Break Skills into Micro Skills and Master One at a Time**
36. **Develop a System or Process You Can Teach**
37. **Host a Live Workshop or Free Training**
38. **Launch a Challenge (e.g., "30-Day Mastery Sprint")**
39. **Write an eBook, Toolkit, or Guide Around Your Expertise**
40. **Use Your Creativity to Solve a Small Real-World Problem**

- Internal Empowerment

41. **Visualize Yourself as the Expert**
42. **Write a Daily Affirmation Around Mastery**
43. **Surround Yourself with High-Performers**

44. **Keep a "Wins List" of Every Step Forward**
45. **Practice Speaking or Writing as the Expert**
46. **Track the Time Spent Daily on Your Craft**
47. **Remove 3 Time Wasters That Steal From Growth**
48. **Ask God (or your Higher Power) for Wisdom in Skill Growth**
49. **Define Your "Skill Identity" in One Powerful Sentence**
50. **Believe That You Are a Solution to Someone's Problem**

PART 2: 50 Ways to Attract Customers to That Skill Set

Once you have built value, you must attract the right audience.

Brand & Visibility

1. **Create a Clear Value Proposition**
2. **Build a One-Page Website or Landing Page**
3. **Use SEO Keywords to Rank in Google/YouTube**
4. **Create a Free Lead Magnet That Solves a Small Problem**
5. **Post Daily/Weekly on One Platform (LinkedIn, IG, TikTok)**
6. **Start a Personal Newsletter**
7. **Host Live Q&A Sessions on Social Media**
8. **Collaborate with Influencers in Your Space**
9. **Get Featured on Podcasts**
10. **Tell Your Story Often**

Content & Education

11. **Teach One Insight Weekly via Social Media**
12. **Create Infographics That Explain Your Process**
13. **Offer a Free Downloadable Guide**
14. **Use Storytelling to Relate to Customer Pain**
15. **Show Before & After Transformations**
16. **Write Blog Posts That Answer Common Questions**
17. **Create a 3-Part Free Video Series**
18. **Showcase Testimonials (Real or Simulated Early Results)**
19. **Offer a Free Audit or Discovery Call**
20. **Teach a 5-Day Challenge or Bootcamp**

Sales & Offers

21. **Create Tiered Offers (Starter, Signature, Premium)**
22. **Use Limited-Time Offers to Create Urgency**
23. **Design a "Done-for-You" or "Done-with-You" Option**
24. **Bundle Your Product/Service with a Bonus**
25. **Offer a Satisfaction Guarantee**
26. **Use Early Adopter Pricing**
27. **Leverage Word of Mouth (Referral Rewards)**
28. **Have a Clear Call-to-Action on All Content**
29. **Build a Sales Funnel**
30. **Create Scarcity: Only Accept 5 Clients/Month**

Outreach & Engagement

31. **Message Ideal Customers with a Personalized Note**

32. **Join Virtual Summits and Speak**
33. **Send a Weekly Value Email (Not Salesy)**
34. **Create a Facebook or WhatsApp Group**
35. **Interview Ideal Clients and Use Their Words in Marketing**
36. **Launch a Mini Course with Upsells**
37. **Start a Podcast About the Problem You Solve**
38. **Offer a "First Time Client Discount"**
39. **Send Personalized Video Messages**
40. **Follow Up 3–5 Times with Warm Leads**

Belief & Social Proof

41. **Post Screenshots of Wins**
42. **Create Customer Case Studies**
43. **Host Live Demos**
44. **Highlight Real-Life Examples**
45. **Display a Waitlist or Client Queue**
46. **Post "Thank You" or "Shout-Outs" Publicly**
47. **Use Scarcity Language: "We're Almost Full"**
48. **Speak on Stages or Guest on Panels**
49. **Offer Free Access in Exchange for Testimonials**
50. **Let Others Share Their Transformation Story**

PART 3: Connect With Your Customer Powerfully

Use this simple "**Connection Formula**":

Heart → Head → Hand

1. **Heart** – Start with *emotion*: "I understand your frustration. I've been where you are."
2. **Head** – Share *logic & solution*: "Here's why this problem happens and how we fix it."
3. **Hand** – Take *action*: Start by setting your SMART Goal

Optional Tracker Template

Revenue Stream	Source Type	Monthly Earnings	Annual Projection	Notes
Book Sales	Amazon/Print	$	$	
Course Sales	Digital	$	$	
Coaching Clients	Service	$	$	
Licensing Content	IP/License	$	$	
Affiliate Partnerships	Referral Income	$	$	
Paid Speaking Engagements	Live Event	$	$	
Subscription Products	Recurring Income	$	$	
Sponsorships	Brand Partnership	$	$	

Journal Pages

Prompt: 'What is already in my hands that I have overlooked?'

Prompt: 'When was a time I solved a problem easily for someone else?'

Prompt: 'What gifts do others consistently recognize in me that I sometimes underestimate?'

Study Session Activities

1. Read Chapter One aloud and underline every phrase that challenges your current mindset.
2. Partner with a study buddy and share your Skill Inventory.
3. Set a timer for 15 minutes and brainstorm 10 creative ways to utilize one of your existing skills.

Reflection Prompts

- What surprised me most about what I already have?
- How have I been underestimating my creative ability?
- What's one courageous action I can take this week using what's already in my hands?

Chapter Two: Atmosphere of Success Blueprint

Chapter Two Focus: Building a Life-Shaping Environment Through Wisdom

Workbook Overview

Your environment mirrors your mindset. In Chapter Two, you learned that wisdom shapes your atmosphere, and your atmosphere shapes your outcomes. This workbook will serve as your blueprint for creating a space, establishing a routine, and developing a support system that sets you up for lasting success. Each section includes diagrams, frameworks, reflection tools, and strategic benchmarks to help you achieve your goals.

Success Atmosphere Components

Success is not an accident—it is created by design. These three pillars shape your environment:

1. Wisdom Inputs – What you read, hear, and think daily.
2. Physical Space – What your environment looks and feels like.
3. Daily Disciplines – The actions and habits you repeat.

[Diagram: Triangle with three corners labeled 'Wisdom Inputs', 'Physical Space', 'Daily Disciplines'. Inside the triangle: 'Creative Growth']

- Wisdom Inputs Tracker

List five sources of wisdom you consume each week. Rate each 1–10 based on how much it inspires creative action.

[Table: Source | Type | Weekly Frequency | Action Level (1–10)]

Environment Audit: Clear the Clutter

Evaluate how aligned your space is with your vision.

[Table: Area | Feeling It Gives | What to Remove | What to Add]

Daily Discipline Designer

Design a daily rhythm rooted in wisdom:

- Morning Routine: [Prayer, Reading, Planning, Reflection]
- Work Flow Anchors: [Block time, Focus hours, Break resets]
- Evening Reset: [Review, Gratitude, Adjustments]

Benchmarks to Inspire Success

These high-impact statistics demonstrate the power of wisdom-based structure:

- 92% of people who implement a morning routine experience greater clarity and productivity.
- 86% of top performers structure their space to limit distraction.
- 5x growth: creators with consistent daily routines see results 5 times faster than those with erratic efforts.

Wisdom-Based Decision Filter

Before you make a significant decision, ask:

- Does this move me closer to my purpose?

- Am I choosing from vision or fear?

- What would a wiser version of me do right now?

[Chart: Decision | Emotion | Wisdom Option | Final Choice]

Weekly Success Map

[Template:]

- Top Goal This Week:

- One Wise Action Daily:

- What I'm Eliminating:

- Support Needed:

- End-of-Week Review: Win + Lesson

Reflection Prompts

- What needs to leave my environment to make room for success?

- Who do I need to learn from consistently?

- What's one wisdom-based habit I can build this month?

- How does my current space reflect the future I want?

Vision Wall Blueprint

Design a physical or digital wall filled with:

- Affirmations

- Goals

- Scriptures

- Inspiring quotes

- Visuals of your desired outcomes

[Illustration: Example layout of a 3x3 vision board grid]

PART 1: 50 IDENTITY + MINDSET TRANSFORMATION CONCEPTS

Each of these inspires inner change and empower real-world success:

1. **Identity is a choice** – You can choose to become who you're called to be.
2. **Mindset Is a Muscle** – The more you stretch it, the stronger it gets.
3. **You are already enough** – Start from acceptance, not a sense of lack.
4. **Belief builds reality** – What you believe, you begin to act upon.
5. **Clarity creates momentum** – When you know who you are, movement becomes easy.
6. **Speak It Before You See It** – Words shape your environment and outcome.
7. **Your Story Matters** – Even your failures can fuel someone else's freedom.
8. **Ownership Begins with Awareness** – You cannot change what you don't acknowledge.
9. **Fear Is Not a Stop Sign** – It's a signal that growth is near.
10. **Courage Comes in Small Steps** – Action builds confidence.
11. **Start Before You're Ready**
12. **Discipline Beats Motivation**
13. **Your Network Reflects Your Self-Concept**
14. **Your Habits Forecast Your Future**
15. **Strategy must back Vision**
16. **Creativity Is a Birthright**
17. **Wealth Follows Value, Not Just Work**
18. **Reject Comparison, Embrace Uniqueness**
19. **Self-Love Fuels Self-Discipline**

20. **Forgive Your Past to Create Your Future**
21. **You Are a Creator, Not Just a Consumer**
22. **Mindset Is the First Investment**
23. **Healing Creates Capacity**
24. **Imagination Is a Preview of Your Potential**
25. **You Are the Brand Before the Product**
26. **Energy Flows Where Focus Goes**
27. **Authenticity Attracts Alignment**
28. **Identity Is More Than a Resume**
29. **Every Decision Reinforces Who You're Becoming**
30. **You Don't Need Permission to Be Powerful**
31. **Ownership Is a Daily Practice**
32. **Scarcity Mindset Limits Legacy**
33. **Self-Worth Precedes Net Worth**
34. **Choose Purpose Over Popularity**
35. **Your Identity Is Not Your Trauma**
36. **What You Tolerate, You Teach**
37. **You Can't Lead Others If You're Lost Yourself**
38. **You're One Aligned Habit Away from Breakthrough**
39. **Your Next Level Requires a New Narrative**
40. **Let Go to Grow**
41. **Mindset + Action = Results**
42. **Faith Fuels Fortitude**
43. **What You Build Builds You Back**
44. **Every Identity Shift Requires Risk**
45. **Work Ethic Reflects Self-Respect**
46. **Knowledge Is Power Only When Applied**
47. **You Are Your First Business**

48. **Don't Just Think Bigger—Believe Bigger**
49. **Identity + Strategy = Destiny**
50. **Purpose-Driven Identity Is Unstoppable**

PART 2: 100 TOOLS TO HELP TRANSFORM IDENTITY INTO REALITY

Below is an outline of what the 100 tools package includes:

A. FRAMEWORKS (20)

- Identity Evolution Ladder
- The "Own It" Self-Worth Pyramid
- Creator Mindset Map
- Daily Decision Dashboard
- Vision-to-Reality Funnel
- 90-Day Creator Blueprint
- 4-Part Wealth Framework (Mindset, Product, Platform, Legacy)
- From Scarcity to Sustainability Model
- Thought > Emotion > Action Cycle
- Core Value Alignment Grid
- Mindset Reset Wheel
- Habits of Ownership Grid
- The "Before & After" Self-Image Matrix
- Vision Board Layout Framework
- Who-You-Are vs What-You-Do Tracker
- Power Routine Map (AM/PM version)

- The “I Create” Affirmation Ladder
- Time Ownership Flow Chart
- Inner Critic to Inner Coach Map
- Confidence Commitment Chart

B. DIAGRAMS + VISUALS (20)

- Wealth Journey Visual Blueprint
- Diamond + Quadrant Life Creator Model
- Identity Venn Diagram (Values, Beliefs, Habits)
- 4-Quadrant Creator Compass
- Action-to-Result Chain
- Wheel of Creator Identity
- Success Staircase
- The Clarity Cone
- Pain to Purpose Path
- Weekly Progress Tracker Wheel
- Fear vs Growth Circle
- Opportunity Filter Matrix
- Thought Detox Map
- Focus Funnel
- Creator Cycle Diagram (Envision > Act > Adjust > Evolve)
- Energy Alignment Chart
- Limiting Belief Crusher Chart
- Revenue Streams Pyramid
- Circle of Control vs Circle of Concern
- Motivation & Momentum Thermometer

C. REFLECTION TOOLS (30)

- Weekly Identity Check-In
- "What I Now Believe" Worksheet
- Who Am I Becoming? Prompts
- Obstacle Ownership Prompts
- Visualize Your Next Level Worksheet
- Core Belief Inventory
- Gratitude Grid
- The "I Am" Rewrite Page
- Daily Creator Journal
- Transformation Trigger List
- What's in My Hands? Reflection Sheet
- Wealth Mindset Audit
- Fear Story Rewriter
- "If I Were Bold..." Reflection
- What Would Future Me Do?
- Daily Decision Scorecard
- Forgiveness Letter (to self)
- Permission Slip Generator
- "What's Draining My Power?" Audit
- Alignment Accountability Sheet
- Commitment to Change Contract
- Celebration Reflection (monthly wins)
- "What Do I Want to Be Known For?"
- Influence Impact Map
- Legacy Letter Draft
- Scarcity to Abundance Rewrite Sheet

- Energy vs Priority Tracker
- Money Story Rewrite
- Personal Rules of Success Sheet
- Weekly Reflection for Identity Growth

D. STRATEGIC BENCHMARKS (30)

- Identity Evolution Tracker
- Mindset Milestone Map
- Daily Habits Tracker (21/45/90 Days)
- Weekly Win Report
- Monthly Vision Execution Sheet
- Dream Activation Scorecard
- Revenue Reality vs Goal Chart
- Progress Pyramid: Foundation > Strategy > Scale
- Network Impact Benchmark
- Creator Confidence Index
- "Belief to Behavior" Scorecard
- Customer/Client Impact Sheet
- Consistency Over Time Chart
- Personal Growth Index
- Values Alignment Checklist
- Inner Dialogue Tracker
- Resilience Report Card
- Mindset Reset Timeline
- Lifestyle Upgrade Index
- Daily Ownership Log

- Weekly Creator Actions Chart
- Focus and Execution Meter
- Vision Execution Heat Map
- Productivity vs Alignment Matrix
- Risk-Tolerance Assessment
- Financial Belief Benchmark
- New Identity Test (Are You Acting Like It?)
- Emotional Intelligence Chart
- Ownership vs Victimhood Audit
- Next Level Blueprint Summary Sheet

FINAL REMARK

This toolkit will be the soul of your movement.
Every visual, chart, and prompt will guide you from "Who am I?" to "I am becoming." It is not just theory—it is measurable, transformational work you must do.

Creativity Is Currency – Chapter Three: Course Material & Workbook

Chapter Three Focus: The Power of Belief

Course Material: Overview

In Chapter Three, you are invited to recognize that belief is the first fuel of every incredible creation. This course module will help you strengthen your belief system, align it with action, and build unstoppable momentum toward your creative goals.

Guided Exercises

Exercise 1: Belief Inventory
- List the beliefs you currently hold about yourself, your creativity, and your potential.

Exercise 2: Belief Upgrade
- Identify one limiting belief you want to replace. Write the new empowering belief you will adopt.

Exercise 3: Daily Belief Activation
- Create a simple morning ritual: Speak aloud three positive beliefs about your creativity every day.

Belief Is the Fuel to Incredible Creation: 50 Real Examples

Belief is the internal engine that powers creativity, innovation, persistence, and results. Without belief, even the best ideas will remain dormant.

Here Are 50 Ways Belief Leads to Creation:

1. Belief helped Thomas Edison invent the light bulb after over 1,000 failures.
2. Belief helped Oprah rise from poverty to become a media mogul.
3. Belief helped Steve Jobs bring Apple back from the brink of collapse.
4. Belief fuels an artist who paints their first canvas.

5. Belief drives a writer to complete their manuscript.
6. Belief empowers an entrepreneur to pitch their startup.
7. Belief fuels a parent to raise strong, confident children.
8. Belief gives a teacher the passion to change a student's life.
9. Belief enables a dancer to express a story through their body.
10. Belief inspires an athlete to break records.
11. Belief fuels a student to apply for scholarships.
12. Belief gave Martin Luther King Jr. the courage to dream.
13. Belief empowers a dreamer to launch a YouTube channel.
14. Belief helps a coach motivate a losing team into a winning one.
15. Belief ignites a speaker to deliver a life-changing message.
16. Belief fuels a baker to turn a home recipe into a business.
17. Belief helps an investor stay consistent through market downturns.
18. Belief allows a person to leave a toxic environment and start fresh.
19. Belief turns a journal entry into a published book.
20. Belief powers a leader to launch a movement.
21. Belief allowed NASA to put a man on the moon.
22. Belief helped inventors create the first airplane.
23. Belief helped a refugee build a multimillion-dollar company.
24. Belief helps a singer perform despite stage fright.
25. Belief enables a volunteer to change someone's world.
26. Belief propels a content creator to build a loyal audience.
27. Belief helped Nelson Mandela survive 27 years in prison.
28. Belief allows someone to learn a new skill at 60 years old.
29. Belief gives someone the courage to try again after failure.
30. Belief enables a person to forgive and begin the healing process.
31. Belief helps someone turn their pain into purpose.
32. Belief helped invent the wheel, fire, and electricity.

33. Belief helps someone apply for a dream job.
34. Belief gives a founder the strength to keep hiring.
35. Belief helps a person say "I can" when others say "you can't."
36. Belief lets someone teach themselves a new language.
37. Belief makes a business start in a garage become global.
38. Belief lets an inventor push forward when no one understands.
39. Belief powers a doctor to find a cure.
40. Belief gives a visionary the drive to launch a non-profit.
41. Belief helps a team complete the project even when they are tired.
42. Belief helps a couple rebuild after heartbreak.
43. Belief allows a pastor to plant a church from scratch.
44. Belief enables a child to say, "I can be anything."
45. Belief helps someone quit a job to pursue a purpose.
46. Belief turns a setback into a setup.
47. Belief builds bridges across cultures and communities.
48. Belief fuels the invention of the Internet.
49. Belief helps someone overcome impostor syndrome.
50. Belief turns impossible into "I'm possible."

---

100 Ways to Strengthen Belief, Align with Desire, and Build Momentum

Here's how the reader can intentionally **strengthen belief**, align with their **dreams**, and maintain **forward motion**:

Identity + Alignment (Mindset)

1. Journal your current beliefs — challenge false ones.

2. Write your new empowering belief daily.
3. Visualize your desired future every morning.
4. Speak affirmations that align with your goal.
5. Create a personal vision statement.
6. Declare your identity out loud: "I am a creator."
7. Rewrite your story from the lens of power.
8. Identify 3 limiting beliefs and destroy them.
9. Replace "I can't" with "How can I?"
10. Study people who reflect the belief you want.
11. Surround yourself with people who share your values and are driven by their beliefs.
12. Remove toxic influences from your life.
13. Create a "Why I Believe" wall or board.
14. Name your new identity and step into it.
15. Develop a morning ritual as a creator.
16. Use your imagination to walk in success now.
17. Invest time in activities that affirm your beliefs.
18. Act "as if" you've already achieved it.
19. Ask yourself: What would the successful version of me do today?
20. Use faith-based scriptures or truths to affirm belief.

Information + Inspiration

21. Read biographies of people you admire.
22. Listen to empowering podcasts daily.
23. Watch one motivational video every morning.
24. Take a course that strengthens your confidence.
25. Learn from mentors who've done it.

26. Study the psychology of success.
27. Read books that expand your vision.
28. Take notes from creative thinkers and leaders.
29. Watch documentaries on breakthrough moments.
30. Join a mastermind or support group.

Action Builds Belief:

31. Take one bold action daily.
32. Complete a micro-win in the morning.
33. Launch a mini project in 7 days.
34. Ask someone to hold you accountable.
35. Share your goal publicly.
36. Track progress with a belief scorecard.
37. Take messy, imperfect action.
38. Write a plan and follow it.
39. Make one scary phone call.
40. Try something outside your comfort zone.

Reinforcement & Feedback:

41. Review your wins weekly.
42. Celebrate each victory, no matter how small.
43. Journal every win to reinforce confidence.
44. Create a "believer's trophy shelf."
45. Ask for testimonials from others you've helped.
46. Reflect on how far you've come.
47. Take feedback as fuel, not failure.
48. Update your affirmations monthly.

49. Reassess goals every 90 days.
50. Build a "belief booster" playlist.

Systems and Habits:

51. Time-block your goals on your calendar.
52. Use habit trackers to stay consistent.
53. Set daily belief-building alarms.
54. Build a morning ritual of mindset + movement.
55. Create weekly review rituals.
56. Plan 90-day sprints.
57. Use reminders to repeat powerful statements.
58. Join belief-boosting challenges.
59. Gamify your progress.
60. Align the environment with your dreams.

Soul + Spirit:

61. Pray or meditate daily.
62. Read spiritual or sacred texts.
63. Practice gratitude every morning.
64. Forgive past mistakes.
65. Write love letters to your future self.
66. Practice silence and stillness.
67. Identify your purpose — revisit often.
68. Speak life over yourself.
69. Connect with like-minded faith builders.
70. Release fear through journaling or worship.

Relationships:

71. Spend time with creators and dreamers.
72. Ask a mentor for guidance.
73. Find a coach or accountability partner.
74. Collaborate with someone aligned.
75. Eliminate doubters from your inner circle.
76. Attend live events that fuel belief.
77. Host a vision night with friends.
78. Talk to someone who's done what you dream of.
79. Start a belief-building group.
80. Share what you're learning.

Reflective Practices:

81. Keep a belief journal.
82. Ask: "What's the best that could happen?"
83. Reflect on your divine design and the unique gifts you possess.
84. Write letters to your future self.
85. Keep a daily "creator log."
86. Track how belief influences your choices.
87. Map out your evolution of beliefs over time.
88. Ask, "Where did I show up boldly today?"
89. Reflect on how your beliefs that affect your relationships.
90. Write out your "I am" list weekly.

Vision Expansion:

91. Dream 10x bigger than today.

92. Create a 10-year vivid vision.
93. Walk through your future house or stage.
94. Print your dream-life photos.
95. Write your obituary from a place of legacy.
96. Reverse-engineer your biggest goal.
97. Visualize your book on a shelf or bestseller list.
98. Create a mock “Future You” interview.
99. Build a “Belief Map” that connects action + purpose.
100. Keep showing up. Believe it again tomorrow.

Action Steps:

1. Identify and reframe one negative belief daily for 7 days.
2. Create a 'Belief Declaration' you say each morning.
3. Surround yourself with three people, books, or environments that reinforce your positive beliefs.
4. Take one small action based on belief, not fear, each week.

Templates:

- Belief Inventory Template: [Current Belief] | [Limiting/Empowering] | [New Belief]
- Belief Declaration Template: 'I believe I can ___ because ___.'
- Weekly Belief Tracker: [Day] | [Positive Belief Affirmed] | [Action Taken Based on Belief]

Monetization Checklist:

- Do I believe I deserve to create wealth through my creativity?
- Am I speaking life over my ideas instead of doubt?

- Have I acted in alignment with my belief in my product, service, or solution?
- Am I marketing and selling from a place of confidence?
- Do I believe there is an audience eager for what I create?

Idea-to-Income Framework (Belief Edition):

Step 1: Believe Your Idea is Needed

Step 2: Build the First Draft Without Fear

Step 3: Launch Before You Feel 'Ready'

Step 4: Sell From a Place of Confidence and Service

Step 5: Reinforce Your Belief Through Wins and Testimonials

Step 6: Expand Your Offer Based on Success Stories

Journal Pages:

Prompt: 'What do I believe about myself as a creator?'

Prompt: 'When was a time my belief created a breakthrough?'

Prompt: 'What belief do I need to strengthen to reach my next level?'

Study Session Activities:

1. Read Chapter Three and circle every statement related to the power of belief.
2. In a group or with a partner, discuss: 'How does belief shape the outcomes we experience?'
3. Create a 'Belief Vision Board' with words and images representing your chosen beliefs.

Reflection Prompts

- How has belief—or lack thereof—shaped my past results?
- What small action can I take this week that proves my belief in my future?
- What are three beliefs I will no longer entertain starting today?

Creativity Is Currency – Chapter: Course Material & Workbook

Chapter Four Focus: Creating Through Pain

Course Material: Overview

In Chapter Four, you are encouraged to recognize that your painful experiences are not roadblocks but raw materials for creative breakthroughs. This course module will help you transform pain into purpose-driven creations that inspire, heal, and build a legacy.

Guided Exercises

Exercise 1: Pain to Purpose Mapping
- Identify one painful experience and list three lessons it taught you.

Exercise 2: Strengths Born From Struggles
- Reflect on how past challenges made you stronger, wiser, or more resourceful.

Exercise 3: Create a Healing Offering
Brainstorm a product, service, or message that could help others who are going through similar struggles.

Dear Reader,

Please don't let your pain become your prison.

You've been through battles no one sees. You've carried weights that bent your back but not your soul. What if I told you that your pain was never meant to break you, but to build you? To shape something inside of you, no easy path ever could?

Pain doesn't disqualify you. It qualifies you.

Your story—your struggle—is not a stop sign. It's a signal. A signal that you're still here, still breathing, still becoming. Every tear has the potential to water your purpose. Every sleepless night can give birth to clarity. Every "no" you've ever heard can fuel the "yes" you were born to provide yourself with.

You're not alone in your pain. And you're not powerless in your purpose.

Use your past as your platform. Use your suffering as a strategy. Use your wounds as wisdom. It's time to own what once owned you.

Let your pain become your power.

100 Examples of Pain Turning into Purpose

Loss & Grief

1. Losing a loved one → Starting a support group for grieving families
2. Divorce → Writing a book on emotional healing

3. Death of a child → Creating a scholarship fund in their honor
4. Miscarriage → Starting a podcast for women navigating loss
5. Terminal illness of a parent → Becoming a hospice advocate
6. Being widowed → Hosting retreats for widows and widowers
7. Losing a sibling → Starting an awareness campaign for prevention
8. Losing a friend to suicide → Creating mental health outreach programs
9. Childhood abuse → Becoming a trauma therapist
10. Abandonment → Building homes for foster youth

Health Struggles

11. Cancer diagnosis → Launching a wellness brand
12. Disability → Becoming a motivational speaker
13. Mental illness → Starting a blog on healing and coping
14. Chronic pain → Creating a wellness app
15. Weight struggles → Becoming a fitness coach
16. Eating disorder → Writing a memoir and coaching others
17. Addiction recovery → Opening a sober living house
18. Recovery from surgery → Creating tools for patient aftercare
19. Living with a rare illness → Advocating for medical research
20. Infertility → Becoming a fertility coach

Rejection & Betrayal

21. Fired from job → Start your own company
22. Denied a promotion → Launching a leadership course
23. Family betrayal → Writing a book on forgiveness
24. Relationship infidelity → Building a marriage support community
25. Not accepted into college → Founding a scholarship fund
26. Bullied → Creating an anti-bullying curriculum

27. Rejected manuscript → Self-publishing a bestseller
28. Losing a business partner → Building something bigger alone
29. Fired unjustly → Becoming a legal advocate for others
30. Passed over for awards → Creating your platform

Financial Struggles

31. Bankruptcy → Teaching financial literacy
32. Poverty → Building generational wealth
33. Foreclosure → Becoming a real estate coach
34. Credit card debt → Launching a debt-free course
35. Student loan debt → Educating on thoughtful financial planning
36. Unpaid internships → Creating paid programs for youth
37. Money mismanagement → Becoming a personal finance blogger
38. Lived on government aid → Teaching how to thrive with little
39. Car repossession → Creating a car buying checklist
40. Scammed → Warning others through public awareness

Career & Business Challenges

41. Laid off → Launching your consulting firm
42. Toxic boss → Creating a workplace culture course
43. Startup failed → Mentoring new entrepreneurs
44. Wrong career path → Becoming a career clarity coach
45. Office harassment → Advocating for safe workplaces
46. No mentorship → Starting mentorship programs
47. Lack of promotion → Helping others break glass ceilings
48. Career burnout → Writing a book on rest & recovery
49. Mistreated as a minority → Speaking on diversity & inclusion
50. Career stagnation → Teaching job pivot strategies

Identity & Belonging

51. Not fitting in → Building your tribe
52. Immigrant story → Inspiring through cultural storytelling
53. Misunderstood faith → Starting interfaith dialogue
54. Gender discrimination → Educating and advocating
55. Racial trauma → Starting equity-based initiatives
56. LGBTQ+ rejection → Hosting safe space groups
57. Foster care system → Becoming a youth advocate
58. Being adopted → Helping others find their roots
59. Cultural barriers → Teaching global leadership
60. Never feeling "enough" → Empowering others to see their worth

Childhood Trauma

61. Grew up in poverty → Teaching wealth building
62. Parent in prison → Mentoring at-risk youth
63. Dysfunctional family → Coaching on healthy boundaries
64. Lived in shelter → Advocating for housing justice
65. Childhood neglect → Becoming a parenting coach
66. Sexual abuse survivor → Creating survivor support circles
67. Grew up in a war zone → Becoming a peacebuilder
68. Generational trauma → Breaking cycles and educating others
69. Had no voice → Becoming a spoken word artist
70. Early orphan → Starting a foundation for orphans

Love, Relationships & Loneliness

71. Serial heartbreak → Writing a dating detox course
72. Toxic friendships → Coaching on emotional boundaries
73. Codependency → Teaching self-worth and independence

74. Loneliness → Creating a thriving community network
75. Being single long-term → Empowering singles with purpose
76. Child estrangement → Healing through community storytelling
77. Difficult in-laws → Hosting communication workshops
78. Long-distance relationships → Teaching digital intimacy
79. Long wait for love → Helping others love themselves first
80. Bad dating experiences → Creating safer dating resources

Personal Failure & Growth

81. Made poor decisions → Teaching decision-making mastery
82. Burned bridges → Coaching on reputation rebuilding
83. Self-sabotage → Creating mindset change programs
84. Procrastination → Launching a productivity planner
85. Negative self-talk → Creating affirmations that heal
86. Failed goals → Teaching goal-reset frameworks
87. Legal trouble → Coaching on clean slates
88. Letting people down → Becoming a trusted guide
89. Quitting too soon → Teaching perseverance
90. Being the black sheep → Becoming the bold leader

Reinvention & Redemption

91. Rock bottom → Becoming a resilience expert
92. Jail time → Becoming a criminal justice reformer
93. Major illness → Creating healing retreats
94. Failed marriage → Hosting relationship recovery programs
95. Homelessness → Starting a transitional housing initiative
96. Midlife crisis → Helping others start again
97. Betrayed by the system → Reforming broken systems

98. Health scare → Promoting preventive health care
99. Felt like a failure → Now empowering champions
100. Silence → Becoming the voice others need

Word to the Reader:

No matter what pain you've endured—emotional, physical, financial, relational—it doesn't define you. What you do with it does.

Let this book be the spark, the strategy, and the support you've been praying for.

Your breakthrough is not despite your pain. It's because of it.

Own it. Create from it. And prosper because of it.

Action Steps:

1. Choose one painful experience and write about the transformation it caused in you.
2. Identify who needs the wisdom you gained through that experience.
3. Develop a simple offer—coaching, a workshop, a guide, a blog post, or a product—that blesses others.
4. Commit to viewing your pain as a platform, not a prison.

Templates

- Pain to Purpose Template: [Painful Event] | [Lesson Learned] | [Creative Idea]
- Strength Through Struggle Template: [Challenge] | [Skill/Strength Gained] | [Potential Application]
- Healing Offer Brainstorm: [Audience] | [Pain Point] | [Solution You Offer]

Monetization Checklist:

- Can my story inspire, educate, or empower others?
- Have I turned my struggle into a solution?
- Is there a group of people currently facing what I have overcome?
Can I create an offer (eBook, coaching, speaking, mentoring) that serves their needs?
- Am I sharing from a healed place, not an open wound?

Idea-to-Income Framework (Pain-to-Purpose Edition):

Step 1: Identify a pain you've overcome.

Step 2: Clarify the wisdom or method that helped you heal or succeed.

Step 3: Design a product, service, or story that delivers hope and tools.

Step 4: Package and position it as a solution.

Step 5: Share authentically with communities who need it.

Step 6: Grow your platform as a voice of healing and transformation.

Journal Pages:

Prompt: 'What past pain still holds untapped lessons for me?'

Prompt: 'How has my greatest struggle strengthened my voice?'

Prompt: 'What message would I deliver to someone facing what I once did?'

Study Session Activities:

1. Read Chapter Four and underline every reference to transformation.
2. Partner Exercise: Share a victory that grew from a painful moment.
3. Group Discussion: 'How can we honor our scars without living in them?'

Reflection Prompts

- What does it mean to 'create through pain' instead of being stuck in it?
- What testimony could my creativity become?
- How will I use my story as a bridge to help others cross into freedom?

Creativity Is Currency – Chapter Five: Course Material & Workbook

Chapter Five Focus: Releasing Fear

Course Material: Overview

Chapter Five encourages you to break free from fear, the invisible barrier that traps creativity. This course module will help you recognize fear for what it is, replace it with action, and move boldly toward the creative future you are called to build.

Guided Exercises

Exercise 1: Fear Inventory
- List of fears currently blocking your creativity, business ideas, or decisions.

Exercise 2: Fear Reframing
- Write the truth that counteracts each fear (e.g., Fear: 'I'm not ready.' Truth: 'Progress is better than perfection.')

Exercise 3: Small Brave Steps
- Choose one fear and list three small, immediate actions you can take to confront it today.

Action Steps:

1. Identify your top 3 creativity-related fears.
2. Reframe each fear with a powerful truth.

3. Take one uncomfortable action per week for the next month.
4. Document and celebrate every small step forward.

Templates:

- Fear Inventory Template: [Fear] | [Truth] | [Next Action]
- Courage Tracker Template: [Date] | [Fear Confronted] | [Action Taken] | [How I Felt After]
- Victory Log Template: [Fear] | [Action] | [Result]

Monetization Checklist:

- Am I allowing fear of failure to stop me from launching my product or service?
Am I visible enough to let others know what I have to offer?
- Have I positioned my creativity as a solution, not just a talent?
- Have I offered my services boldly to people who need them?
- Have I celebrated progress, even when it's small?

Idea-to-Income Framework (Fearless Edition):

Step 1: Name the fear that's stopping you.

Step 2: Write the truth that overrides that fear.

Step 3: Choose the smallest courageous action you can take now.

Step 4: Deliver value imperfectly but consistently.

Step 5: Grow stronger by tracking wins and feedback.

Step 6: Scale your offerings as confidence expands.

FEAR: Recognize It. Replace It. Transform It.

“Fear is not your enemy. It’s your invitation to grow.”

What Is Fear?

Fear is a protective mechanism rooted in uncertainty. It's not failure—but the anticipation of failure—that holds you back. Fear disguises itself as logic, procrastination, perfectionism, and even false humility. If you don't recognize fear for what it is, it will quietly rob you of your destiny.

25 Examples of What Fear Looks Like:

These are not just feelings—they're roadblocks:

1. "What if I'm not good enough?"

2. Overthinking every decision.

3. Constantly comparing yourself to others.

4. Avoiding risks, even calculated ones.

5. Waiting for the "perfect" time.

6. Talking yourself out of new ideas.

7. "I don't have enough experience."

8. Thinking small to avoid failure.

9. Letting others' opinions control your vision.

10. Delaying the launch of your product or service.

11. Fear of being seen or judged.

12. Giving up after one setback.

13. Fearing rejection more than desiring growth.

14. Holding on to a steady job you've outgrown.

15. Discounting your prices out of insecurity.

16. Believing wealth is for "other people."

17. Refusing help or feedback.

18. Not finishing what you start.

19. Confusing humility with hiding.

20. Doubting your creativity.

21. Struggling to celebrate your wins.

22. Avoiding money conversations.

23. Being busy to avoid being productive.

24. Staying in preparation mode.

25. Focusing on what could go wrong.

Replace Fear with Bold Action – 25 Transformations

Now shift fear into *forward movement*:

1. Say "yes" before you're ready.
2. Launch messy instead of waiting for perfect.
3. Speak your vision out loud every day.
4. Set one non-negotiable creative goal per week.
5. Surround yourself with action-takers.

6. Raise your prices—and believe in the value you offer.
7. Write down your wins daily.
8. Ask someone for feedback today.
9. Take one bold step outside your comfort zone.
10. Replace "what if I fail?" with "what if I win?"
11. Create before you consume.
12. Build while scared—bravery is action, not absence of fear.
13. Make one public commitment to your audience.
14. Remind yourself of what you survived before.
15. Visualize your highest self and act from that place.
16. Put a date on your product launch.
17. Record a video or podcast to share your story.
18. Apply for an opportunity that stretches you.
19. Write and send that bold pitch.
20. Tell someone your dream, even if it's scary.
21. Invest in your personal growth.
22. Take a 30-minute walk to clear fear and refocus.
23. Say "no" to what drains your creativity.
24. Keep a fear journal—and write a solution beside it.
25. Celebrating fear means you're growing.

10 Ways to Turn Fear into Success

These practical examples show how you can push forward:

1. Start your first blog.
2. Publish your first YouTube video.

3. Host a 5-person webinar.
4. Self-publish your eBook.
5. Build a simple landing page.
6. Create your first product mockup.
7. Launch your coaching program.
8. Run a Facebook ad.
9. Reach out to a podcast for a guest spot.
10. Share your story on social media.

From Fear to Flow: A Call to Boldness

Every fear you face is proof you're near the edge of a breakthrough. Don't retreat—advance. Don't suppress your creativity—express it. And don't wait—**build boldly.**

Fear never truly goes away. But it always shrinks when faced.

Journal Pages

Prompt: 'What is the biggest fear holding back my next level?'

Prompt: 'When have I been brave before? What did I learn from that experience?'

Prompt: 'What could happen if I acted boldly for the next 30 days?'

Study Session Activities

1. Read Chapter Five and underline every reference to courage and action.
2. Share with a partner: 'A fear I'm ready to face and the truth I will replace it with.'
3. Group Challenge: 'What would you do if you knew fear couldn't win?' Make a public commitment.

Reflection Prompts

- How is fear costing me opportunities, impact, or income?
- What would my life look like if fear had no say in my creativity?
- What bold step will I take in the next 24 hours?

Creativity Is Currency – Chapter Six: Course Material & Workbook

Chapter Six Focus: Starting Small, Dreaming Big

Course Material: Overview

Chapter Six encourages you to understand the power of starting where you are—with small beginnings and bold visions. This course module will help you embrace humble starts while building toward massive, life-changing outcomes.

Guided Exercises

Exercise 1: Small Start Inventory
- List five small steps you can take this week toward a bigger creative goal.

Exercise 2: Dream Expansion
- Write a vivid vision of where your creativity could take you in 1 year, 5 years, and 10 years.

Exercise 3: Celebrate Small Wins
- Identify and celebrate three recent wins connected to your creativity, no matter how small they seem.

Start Where You Are: The Power of Urgency

Dear Reader,

You don't need to wait. You don't need to have it all figured out. You don't need more time, more degrees, or more money to begin. The most important resource you need is already within you—your **creativity**, your **courage**, and your **willingness to start now**.

Waiting delays your purpose. Starting now creates momentum.

It's not about perfection, it's about movement. Every step taken in purpose beats standing still in fear. When you begin, no matter how small, you build the muscle of belief, the vision of your future, and the life you were created to live.

You must begin now, boldly, even if it's messy, because waiting for ideal conditions is how dreams die quietly.

50 Examples of Small Beginnings + Bold Visions

Small Beginning	Bold Vision It Leads To
1. Write one page a day	Publishing a bestselling book
2. Selling one digital product	Scaling to a 7-figure course empire
3. Speaking to 3 people about your idea	Launching a sold-out live event
4. Building a one-page website	Creating a powerful brand platform
5. Drawing one design	Launching a global product line
6. Hosting a free webinar	Building a coaching empire
7. Offering free services to 1 client	Attracting premium-paying clients
8. Making one video	Growing into a high-paid influencer
9. Creating a mission statement	Starting a non-profit that changes lives

10. Budgeting $10/week to invest	Building generational wealth
11. Reading one book	Transforming into a thought leader
12. Journaling your goals	Becoming a bestselling author & speaker
13. Posting value on social media	Growing a thriving community
14. Practicing a new skill 15 mins a day	Becoming a master in your industry
15. Building one product sample	Owning a product-based business
16. Asking one mentor for guidance	Building a powerful network
17. Organizing one workshop	Launching a coaching institute
18. Researching business licenses	Starting a legitimate company
19. Hosting a book club	Becoming a literary thought leader
20. Starting a daily prayer/meditation practice	Gaining internal clarity and wisdom
21. Volunteering time or talent	Creating a social impact brand
22. Creating one worksheet	Building a transformative workbook series
23. Recording voice notes of ideas	Launching a podcast heard worldwide
24. Testing one small ad	Running multi-channel ad campaigns
25. Studying successful entrepreneurs	Becoming one
26. Mapping out your financial goals	Reaching financial freedom
27. Creating your first lead magnet	Building a high-converting sales funnel
28. Buying one domain name	Launching your online brand
29. Hosting a virtual meetup	Building a global mastermind
30. Writing a daily affirmation	Rewiring your belief system
31. Sharing your testimony	Becoming a motivational speaker

32. Investing in your first tool/platform	Building a tech-enabled company
33. Asking customers for feedback	Creating better products that scale
34. Building one revenue stream	Creating multiple passive incomes
35. Pitching one idea to someone	Getting published or funded
36. Hosting a Q&A live	Launching a mentorship community
37. Organizing your workspace	Cultivating creative productivity
38. Taking an online course	Getting certified and expanding your services
39. Starting with your phone	Creating a visual content brand
40. Saving your first $100	Investing in assets
41. Taking a walk to clear your mind	Gaining divine clarity
42. Visualizing your ideal life	Manifesting the vision
43. Saying "yes" to one opportunity	Opening doors of favor and influence
44. Writing down your legacy	Beginning your estate and legacy plan
45. Learning about copyrights & IP	Protecting and profiting from your creations
46. Building your logo and brand colors	Launching a recognizable brand
47. Hiring a coach or mentor	Accelerating your success trajectory
48. Releasing the fear of judgment	Gaining the boldness to lead
49. Creating your first offer	Building a scalable product suite
50. Sharing your purpose aloud	Attracting your destiny connections

Tracking Growth: From Small Start to Big Success

Stage	What You're Doing	What It Looks Like	Stage
Start	Learning + Taking Action	Writing, building, talking, creating	Start
Grow	Iterating + Improving	Testing offers, building an audience	Grow
Scale	Leveraging + Expanding	Systems, team, high-ticket offers	Scale
Impact	Influencing + Leading	Book tours, courses, legacy programs	Impact

Call to Action:

- **Pick one small beginning today.**
- **Write down your bold vision.**
- **Take action before the end of the day.**

You don't need to know all the steps.
You need to take the first one.

Today's action becomes tomorrow's breakthrough.

Are you ready to turn what's in your hands into wealth?

Let's build it together.

Action Steps

1. Commit to taking one small action every day for 30 days.
2. Create a Dream Board or Vision Statement to keep your big goals in sight.
3. Build 'Mini-Goals' that connect small actions to bigger dreams.
4. Share one small win publicly weekly to build confidence and momentum.

Templates

- Small Start Action Plan Template: [Action] | [Start Date] | [End Goal]
- Dream Expansion Template: [1 Year Dream] | [5 Year Dream] | [10 Year Dream]
- Small Wins Log: [Date] | [Small Win] | [What It Means for My Journey]

Monetization Checklist

- Have I created a small offer or product that meets an immediate need?
- Am I treating my small projects with the same seriousness as my big dreams?
- Am I building a community or audience before I feel ready?
- Have I planned a roadmap from my first sale to my big business vision?
- Am I consistent even when the results are small?

Idea-to-Income Framework (Start Small, Scale Big Edition)

Step 1: Launch a Starter Offer (small eBook, mini-course, workshop)

Step 2: Gather Real-World Feedback

Step 3: Refine Your Offer and Expand Value

Step 4: Build a Consistent Client or Customer Base

Step 5: Layer Bigger Offers and Experiences Over Time

Step 6: Scale Systematically Using Your Success Foundation

Journal Pages

Prompt: 'What small beginning am I willing to celebrate today?'

Prompt: 'Where could small, consistent actions lead me over the next 12 months?'

Prompt: 'What part of my big dream excites me the most—and how can I start moving toward it now?'

Study Session Activities

1. Read Chapter Six and highlight references to small beginnings or consistent growth.
2. Partner Activity: Share one small beginning and one big dream, and encourage each other to work towards achieving them.
3. Group Challenge: Set a 30-Day Small Action Challenge together.

Reflection Prompts

- Why is it powerful to start small?
- What would happen if I remained consistent for one year?
- How will I honor the small beginnings God has placed before me?

Creativity Is Currency – Chapter Seven: Course Material & Workbook

Chapter Seven Focus: Building for Others

Course Material: Overview

In Chapter Seven, you are encouraged to shift your focus from creating for yourself to building solutions, services, and products that serve others. This module teaches you to view your creativity as a gift meant to bless people, solve real problems, and build a lasting legacy.

Guided Exercises

Exercise 1: Audience Discovery

- Identify three groups of people who could benefit from your gifts, skills, or story.

Exercise 2: Service Mapping

- For each group identified, list a specific problem you can help them solve.

Exercise 3: Mission Statement Draft

- Write a short mission statement focused on serving others with your creativity.

Action Steps

1. Research your target audience's most significant needs, challenges, and goals.
2. Design a small offer, resource, or service that helps solve one specific problem.
3. Test your solution by offering it to a few people for free or at a discount.
4. Gather testimonials to validate your impact and refine your offer.

"Creator of Impact: From Self-Focus to Solution Builder"

Goal:

To help you embrace your *creative power* by shifting your focus from internal struggles or desires to becoming **problem-solvers** who build meaningful, impactful offerings for others. This creates purpose, profitability, and legacy.

Core Philosophy:

"You weren't just born to dream — you were born to *design solutions* that make life better for someone else."

PROGRAM STRUCTURE

STEP 1: Mindset Shift — From "What Do I Want?" to "Whose Problem Can I Solve?"

Daily Mantra:
"The moment I create value for others, I create a life of meaning for myself."

Have the reader journal:

- Who do I feel called to serve?

- What common struggle or question do I keep seeing in my circle or community?
- How can I use my knowledge, talent, or story to help solve this?

PART 1: 50 Examples of Turning Creativity Into Products That Benefit Others

Example	Description
1. Online course	Teach what you know to solve a recurring issue.
2. Journal planner	Create a system for productivity, mindset, or vision.
3. Coaching program	Help others navigate challenges you've already overcome.
4. Mobile app	Develop a tool that streamlines a complex task.
5. eBook	Answer a common question in your industry.
6. Podcast	Build conversations that educate and inspire.
7. Web platform	Connect people in need with mentors or service providers.

Example	Description
8. Digital templates	Provide plug-and-play designs or forms.
9. Financial workbook	Help others understand the concepts of money and wealth creation.
10. Vision board kit	Inspire clarity and direction.
11. Home organization guide	Create a step-by-step life-simplification system.
12. Relationship journal	Help couples grow in love and communication.
13. Mental health tracker	Create a tool for reflection and self-care.
14. Motivational YouTube series	Serve by speaking life weekly.
15. "From Pain to Power" course	Transform personal pain into a teaching tool.
16. Generational wealth seminar	Teach legacy and stewardship.
17. Prayer and affirmation cards	Encourage spiritual growth and mental peace.
18. Accountability group	Create structure and consistency for goal-setters.
19. Habit-tracking tool	Help others stick to what they start.
20. Wellness planner	Combine mental, physical, and emotional goals.
21. Subscription box	Curate themed solutions monthly.
22. Resume builder service	Help job seekers land better roles.

Example	Description
23. Single parents' support guide	Offer actionable advice and community.
24. Time management system	Help people reclaim their day.
25. Masterclass on "Solving Problems Through Creativity"	Educate on creating offers.

PART 2: 50 Real Problems to Solve + Legacy-Driven Offers You Can Build

These are issues people PAY to solve:

What bothers you so much that you can't ignore it? That may be your assignment.

Problem	Legacy-Building Offer
1. Stress and anxiety	Create a calming journal with routines.
2. Lack of purpose	Build a course on finding one's calling.
3. Financial mismanagement	Create a budgeting toolkit.
4. Burnout	Launch a restorative retreat.
5. Leadership gap in youth	Mentor program or bootcamp.
6. Digital overload	Build an offline creativity kit.
7. Low confidence	Develop a self-worth workshop.
8. Poor communication	Offer a conversation guide system.
9. Marital tension	Build an emotional connection journal.

Problem	Legacy-Building Offer
10. Inconsistent faith	Create a daily spiritual growth guide.
11. Career stagnation	Help retool resumes + LinkedIn presence.
12. Legacy confusion	Teach estate planning and legacy mapping.
13. Self-doubt	Launch an "Unstoppable Confidence" series.
14. Overwhelm	Offer task-organizing and planning tools.
15. Low literacy in the community	Create reading programs or apps.
16. Entrepreneurship fear	Start a support group with action steps.
17. Health neglect	Build a 30-day lifestyle transformation.
18. Imposter syndrome	Create a mindset reframe workbook.
19. Underemployment	Teach creative side hustles.
20. Emotional trauma	Offer storytelling-based healing circles.
21. No support system	Launch community connection groups.
22. Generational curses	Create a curriculum to shift family outcomes.
23. Lack of creative direction	Host vision board and life design sessions.
24. Book writing overwhelm	Offer a step-by-step writing system.
25. Poor branding	Launch a brand identity starter kit.

Call to Action:

"You are a creator, not just of ideas, but of outcomes. It's time to stop holding your gift hostage and start solving problems that build a legacy."

Templates

- Audience Discovery Template: [Audience Group] | [Problem They Face] | [Solution I Can Offer]
- Service Mapping Template: [Skill/Product] | [Need It Solves] | [Benefit for Others]
- Mission Statement Template: 'I create ___ to serve ___ by helping them ___.'

Monetization Checklist

- Am I creating a real solution for a real group of people?
- Is my offer positioned to meet a pressing need?
- Have I communicated the benefits, not just the features?
- Have I collected feedback from real users to validate my offer?
- Am I consistently improving based on service, not just sales?

Idea-to-Income Framework (Service-First Edition)

Step 1: Identify a Group You Can Serve

Step 2: Understand Their Problems Deeply

Step 3: Build a Simple, Service-Oriented Offer

Step 4: Deliver Value Generously to Build Trust

Step 5: Monetize Through Referrals, Testimonials, and Improved Offers

Step 6: Scale by Solving Bigger Problems or Serving Bigger Audiences

Journal Pages

Prompt: 'Who needs what I have to offer?'

Prompt: 'What problem do I feel most called to solve for others?'

Prompt: 'How can I serve others better through my creativity today?'

Study Session Activities

1. Read Chapter Seven and highlight every statement related to service and audience-building.
2. Group Activity: Identify a problem in your community and brainstorm creative solutions to address it.
3. Partner Challenge: Draft a mini-offer together that addresses a single need for a specific individual.

Reflection Prompts

- How does shifting my focus from myself to others transform my creativity?
- What legacy will I leave through serving others with my talents?

What is the next step I can take today to create something that brings joy to people?

How to Protect Your Income Once You've Created It

"The wealth you build must be shielded with wisdom, structure, and foresight. Protect it like a fortress, or risk losing what you've created." — David Toliver

Categories of Protection

We'll break this into five key categories:

1. **Legal & Structural Protection**
2. **Tax Efficiency**
3. **Smart Investments**
4. **Insurance & Risk Management**
5. **Lifestyle, Legacy, and Discipline**

1. Legal & Structural Protection

1. **Create an LLC or Corporation**
   – Separate your personal and business liabilities.
2. **Use Holding Companies**
   – Shield assets behind a parent company.
3. **Trademark Your Brand**
   – Secure your intellectual property and identity.
4. **Copyright Your Content**
   – Protect written, visual, or digital assets.
5. **Sign Contracts for Every Deal**
   – Protect yourself legally in all partnerships.
6. **Hire a Business Attorney**
   – Review every agreement before signing.
7. **Get a CPA or Financial Advisor**
   – Help structure your income correctly.

8. **Create an Estate Plan**

   – Direct where your assets go in life or death.

9. **Set Up a Trust**

   – Protect your family, assets, and business.

10. **Create an NDA (Non-Disclosure Agreement)**

    – When sharing ideas, always protect them.

---

2. Tax Efficiency

1. **Set Up S-Corp or Tax-Efficient Entity**

   – Reduce self-employment taxes.

2. **Track Every Expense**

   – Use tools like QuickBooks or Wave.

3. **Hire a Tax Strategist**

   – Learn to plan, not just file taxes.

4. **Use Home Office Deduction**

   – Deduct the square footage of your workspace.

5. **Deduct Business Travel**

   – Write off trips tied to your business.

6. **Contribute to a SEP IRA or Solo 401(k)**

   – Shelter income for retirement.

7. **Create a Charitable Giving Strategy**

   – Give generously while reducing taxes.

8. **Write Off Professional Education**

   – Books, seminars, and coaching can be deducted.

9. **Depreciate Assets**

   – If you own property or equipment, use depreciation rules.

10. **Hire Your Children or Spouse**

    – Keep income in the family, tax efficiently.

3. Smart Investments

1. **Diversify Your Income Streams**

   – Don't rely on one source alone.
2. **Invest in Index Funds**

   – Low-risk, long-term strategy.
3. **Buy Real Estate**

   – Generate cash flow + asset growth.
4. **Use a 770 Account (Indexed Universal Life Insurance)**

   – Tax-free growth and withdrawals.
5. **Set Aside Emergency Savings (6–12 months)**

   – Always be protected in downturns.
6. **Dollar-Cost Average Your Investments**

   – Stay consistent regardless of the market.
7. **Buy into Tangible Assets (Art, Gold, Land)**

   – Real value never disappears.
8. **Invest in Your Education**

   – No investment beats self-growth.
9. **Have an Opportunity Fund**

   – Cash ready to invest when deals come.
10. **Create a Profit First System**

    – Allocate profits before paying expenses.

4. Insurance & Risk Management

1. **Buy Disability Insurance**
   – Protect your income if you can't work.
2. **Purchase Life Insurance**
   – Leave a legacy, not a burden.
3. **Use Umbrella Insurance**
   – Extra protection beyond standard coverage.
4. **Insure Your Business Assets**
   – Protect inventory, office equipment, and digital tools.
5. **Get Errors & Omissions Insurance**
   – For coaches, consultants, or service providers.
6. **Cybersecurity Protection**
   – Protect your online presence and data.
7. **Backup Your Data Weekly**
   – Use cloud and external drives.
8. **Get Legal Insurance Plans**
   – Affordable access to attorneys on retainer.
9. **Automate Identity Monitoring**
   – Prevent fraud and credit damage.
10. **Create Redundancy in Income Streams**
    – Build "income insurance" through diversification.

---

5. Lifestyle, Legacy, and Financial Discipline

1. **Automate Savings**
   – Pay yourself first without thinking.

2. **Live Below Your Means**
   – Don't let lifestyle creep steal your future.
3. **Use a Budgeting System (50/30/20 Rule)**
   – Track wants, needs, and investments.
4. **Give Generously, But Strategically**
   – Vet charities and causes to avoid waste.
5. **Create a Generational Wealth Plan**
   – What happens after you?
6. **Use a Wealth Dashboard (Spreadsheet or App)**
   – See everything in one place.
7. **Invest in Your Brand**
   – Protect your public reputation.
8. **Journal of Financial Decisions**
   – Track wins and lessons learned.
9. **Practice Gratitude Over Greed**
   – This keeps you grounded and generous.
10. **Review Quarterly Goals**
   – Income growth, protection, and freedom checkpoints.

Income Protection Tracker – [Downloadable Template Available Upon Request]

Revenue Stream	Monthly Income	Year-To-Date	Notes / Risk Level
Book Sales	$	$	

Revenue Stream	Monthly Income	Year-To-Date	Notes / Risk Level
Masterclasses	$	$	
Licensing	$	$	
Speaking Engagements	$	$	
Courses	$	$	
Affiliate Commissions	$	$	
Membership/Subscriptions	$	$	
Merchandising	$	$	
Sponsored Content	$	$	
Consulting Services	$	$	

Track this month to stay aligned with your freedom goals.

Encouragement

"You worked hard for your income. Now work wisely to preserve it. The same creativity that built your success will guard your legacy—if you lead it with intention."

— David Toliver

50 Legacy of Influence and Wealth Examples

Family Impact

1. Funding your children's and grandchildren's education debt-free.
2. Creating a family scholarship fund in your name.
3. Buying property to keep in the family for generations.
4. Leaving behind a portfolio of rental homes that generate passive income.
5. Creating a trust fund to manage wealth and distribute it wisely.
6. Teaching your children entrepreneurship by involving them in the family business.
7. Documenting and sharing your story, values, and family history.
8. Setting up life insurance policies to transfer generational wealth.
9. Modeling emotional intelligence and leadership for your children.
10. Hosting annual family legacy retreats focused on vision and purpose.

Business & Entrepreneurship:

11. Building a successful company that your children can inherit or run.
12. Publishing a book that teaches timeless wealth-building principles.
13. Licensing your intellectual property for passive income.
14. Creating a software, app, or product that solves a recurring problem.
15. Building an online course that generates income long after you're gone.
16. Training others in your field and passing on your expertise.
17. Launching a family foundation or philanthropic fund.
18. Opening a community co-working or innovation center.
19. Creating generational income streams through franchising or licensing.
20. Becoming a thought leader whose content lives on for years.

Education & Mentorship:

21. Mentoring 100 young leaders who each build their legacy.
22. Creating a curriculum for schools to teach creative entrepreneurship.

23. Donating books or tools to libraries in underserved communities.
24. Launching a speaker series or masterclass to inspire others.
25. Endowing a university chair or scholarship in your field.
26. Recording a podcast or video series to mentor people long-term.
27. Starting a youth mentorship nonprofit in your hometown.
28. Hosting creative empowerment workshops for teens and young adults.
29. Helping others become financially literate and own their creativity.
30. Launching a school of influence focused on legacy and mindset.

Community & Global Change:

31. Building a wellness or resource center in an underfunded community.
32. Supporting community gardens, food co-ops, or entrepreneurship hubs.
33. Partnering with local governments to improve education or housing.
34. Funding innovation labs or incubators in minority communities.
35. Empowering other creators and business owners with startup capital.
36. Donating to causes aligned with your personal mission and faith.
37. Partnering with churches or organizations to build training programs.
38. Supporting mothers, fathers, or students with grants and coaching.
39. Rebuilding a school or hospital in your hometown.
40. Sponsoring a global campaign aligned with your values.

Identity, Mindset & Personal Growth:

41. Leading your family spiritually and financially with wisdom.
42. Embodying a mindset of generosity, faith, and discipline.
43. Being remembered as someone who broke the cycle of poverty.
44. Changing your family's narrative by stepping into abundance.
45. Teaching others to monetize their gifts and build meaningful lives.

46. Showing that healing, wholeness, and prosperity are possible.
47. Creating a journal or workbook that your descendants can use to grow.
48. Becoming known as a visionary who impacted generations.
49. Living a life of integrity, faith, and purpose.
50. Inspiring others to believe they can own their creativity and future.

Reflection:

Pick 3–5 of these examples and journal on:

- What would this look like in my life?
- How will my family be impacted?
- What step can I take today to begin this legacy?

A Joyful Send-Off: You Are Ready

Dear Reader,

As you close the final pages of *Creativity Is Currency*, know this truth with all your heart: **You are now fully equipped**. You've taken the journey through the power of your own ideas, beliefs, and untapped potential. What lies ahead of you is not uncertainty, **but opportunity**.

This book was written for dreamers and doers like you—for those who believe that creativity is more than just a concept—it's a calling. And now, **you are ready** to answer that call. You've explored and embraced 15 core transformational topics that are now the cornerstone of your new beginning:

1. Owning Your Creativity

2. Developing a Wealth Identity
3. Embracing the Creator Mindset
4. Mastering the Power of Belief
5. Building with What's In Your Hands
6. Activating Wisdom for Daily Decision-Making
7. Creating Systems That Sustain
8. Learning to Serve and Solve Problems
9. Creating Income Through Value
10. Building a Brand With Meaning
11. Marketing With Clarity and Confidence
12. Developing Readiness to Serve a Market
13. Protecting Your Wealth and Legacy
14. Giving With Purpose and Power
15. Becoming the Person Who Can Receive

With these truths in hand, you have the **tools, vision, and resilience** to design your life, your business, and your future. You are no longer waiting for permission. You are no longer wondering if you're enough.

You are the creator. The innovator. The leader.

You now have the clarity to make courageous decisions, the skill set to take impactful action, and the wisdom to walk in alignment with your purpose.

So we say: **Congratulations!** You've made it to the starting line of your next chapter—and we are cheering you on as you begin. May this book continue to light your path, spark your imagination, and guide you toward **abundant success**.

Thank you for allowing this journey to be part of your story. We hope it brought you joy, revelation, and a bold new perspective on what's possible.

With creative power and unwavering belief in your greatness,
—The Creativity Is Currency Team
David Toliver, Author

Appendix: Tools, Resources & Study Aids

You've built wealth. Now build worth. You've gained power. Now give a purpose. You've walked your journey. Now light the way for someone else.

The world is waiting for your generosity. Don't delay. You are the answer to someone's prayer. Let your legacy begin today.

Now go—be the light. Be the answer. Be the blessing.

Your Guide to Deepen the Journey, Multiply Your Impact, and Leave a Legacy

A. Recommended Reading & Resources

Books That Expand Your Wealth, Wisdom, and Leadership Mindset

The book: **www.theempoweredcreators.com.com/book**

2. Free Introduction Class: **www.theempoweredcreators.com/starter**

3. $99 Signature Class **www.theempoweredcreators.com/blueprint**

4. $5,000 Premium Progress **www.theempoweredcreators.com/legacy**

5. $10,000 Elite Offer **www.theempoweredcreators.com/accelerator**

https://www.theempoweredcreators.com/creative-ideas-into-cash
https://www.theempoweredcreators.com/workbook

Scan the QR Code Below to Get *Creativity Is Currency: How To Turn Your Ideas Into Wealth*

www.ingramcontent.com/pod-product-compliance
Lightning Source LLC
LaVergne TN
LVHW082357200926
848481LV00012B/3592
9798349587597